ZOO ANIMALS
IN THE WILD

GORILLA

JINNY JOHNSON
ILLUSTRATED BY MICHAEL WOODS

A⁺
Smart Apple Media

Published by Smart Apple Media
2140 Howard Drive West, North Mankato, Minnesota 56003

Designed by Helen James
Illustrated by Michael Woods

Photographs by Robert E. Barber, Corbis (Karl Ammann, Yann Arthus-Bertrand, Tom Brakefield, Gallo Images, Darrell Gulin, Martin Harvey, KENT NEWS & PICTURE/CORBIS SYGMA, Joe McDonald, Carmen Redondo, Kevin Schafer, FORESTIER YVES/CORBIS SYGMA), Wildlife Conservation Society (D. DeMello)

Printed and bound in Thailand

Library of Congress Cataloging-in-Publication Data

Johnson, Jinny.
Gorilla / by Jinny Johnson.
p. cm. — (Zoo animals in the wild)
ISBN 1-58340-642-5
1. Gorilla—Juvenile literature. I. Title.

QL737.P96J57 2005
599.884—dc22   2004059966

First Edition

9 8 7 6 5 4 3 2 1

Contents

Gorillas 4

At home in the wild 6

At home in the zoo 8

On the move 10

A gorilla's day 12

Finding food 14

Family life 16

Keeping in touch 18

Gorilla babies 20

Growing up 22

Playtime 24

Leaving home 26

Gorilla fact file 28

Glossary 30

Index 32

Gorillas

Gorillas are the biggest of all the apes. They're much larger than chimpanzees and orangutans. But gorillas are peaceful animals. They eat plants, not other creatures.

A full-grown male gorilla weighs two to three times as much as a full-grown man. Female gorillas are smaller—about half the size of males. A gorilla has a hairy body and no tail. Its arms are longer than its legs. Its skin is black, and it has deep brown eyes. On a gorilla's nose are lots of little folds and wrinkles. No two gorillas have exactly the same nose pattern.

Zoo gorillas are usually a little heavier than wild gorillas. They have richer food and don't get as much exercise as animals living in the wild.

 A male gorilla is much bigger than a female gorilla and has a high, dome-shaped head.

Each gorilla's "nose print" is unique, just like a human's fingerprints.

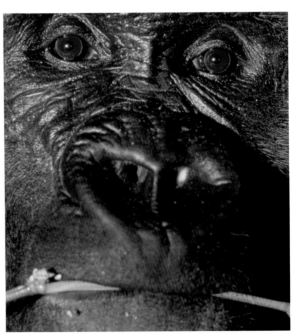

At home in the wild

Wild gorillas live in tropical forests in Africa. It is always hot in these forests, and there is a lot of rain, so there are plenty of fresh plants for gorillas to eat year-round.

There are two main types of gorillas—western lowland gorillas and eastern lowland gorillas. They live in separate areas of forest hundreds of miles apart. There is also a special group of eastern lowland gorillas that lives high in the mountains. These gorillas are known as mountain gorillas and are now very rare. There are no mountain gorillas living in zoos.

A western lowland gorilla takes a break from feeding.

 A pair of mountain gorillas in their mountaintop home.

At home in the zoo

Gorillas live in families in the wild, so the best zoos keep a group of gorillas together. That way, they don't get lonely or bored.

A gorilla's home in the zoo needs to have places where young animals can climb and play, as well as areas where the animals can get away from each other when they want to. There also needs to be outdoor space where they can exercise.

Zoo gorillas are happiest if they have a large enclosure with plenty of space to move around in.

At night, zoo gorillas go into their indoor sleeping areas and make warm beds out of hay. They may also have nesting platforms or even hammocks to sleep in.

A male gorilla gets comfortable for a daytime nap.

Zoo gorillas live longer than animals in the wild. The oldest known gorilla lived at the Philadelphia Zoo. He lived until he was 54 years old. Wild gorillas usually live only 30 years or so.

A climbing frame keeps young zoo gorillas entertained.

9

On the move

Gorillas usually walk on all fours. Sometimes they stand up to reach plants, and they can walk and run upright for a short distance— usually not more than about 60 feet (18 m), or less than the length of a tennis court.

Gorillas spend most of their time on the ground. They can climb trees, but they don't swing from branch to branch like chimpanzees do. Gorillas usually climb only to reach fruit.

As it moves, a gorilla leans on its knuckles, not on the palms of its hands.

Gorillas in the zoo need to be encouraged to move around in their enclosure so they don't get bored—or too heavy! Keepers sometimes hide food around the animals' home for them to find.

Gorillas don't like water very much, and they can't swim. But they will sometimes wade into water to pick plants to eat.

Young and female gorillas are much better than males at climbing trees because they are not as heavy.

A gorilla's day

Gorillas usually wake up at sunrise.
They spend the morning moving slowly
around their home area, feeding as they go.

Around midday, when the sun feels the hottest, they stop for a rest. The grown-ups may sit and groom before taking a little nap while the young play.

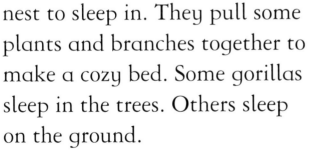

A gorilla makes a new nest every night.

After their nap, the gorillas set off to feed again until dusk. They find a place to spend the night, and each gorilla makes a nest to sleep in. They pull some plants and branches together to make a cozy bed. Some gorillas sleep in the trees. Others sleep on the ground.

A family of mountain gorillas relaxes for several hours in the middle of the day.

Gorillas in the Moscow Zoo in Russia have televisions in their enclosure. The keepers believe that watching films about gorillas and monkeys in the wild gives the zoo gorillas something to do and keeps them happy and interested.

Finding food

Gorillas are vegetarians, which means they feed on plants. They eat huge amounts of leaves and stems from many different plants, including wild celery and bamboo. They also eat berries, fruits, roots, and grasses. Gorillas may look big and fierce, but the only animals they eat are tiny ants and termites.

Because they eat so much, gorillas need to keep moving so they don't eat up all the plants in an area. They need to let some plants grow more leaves and fruit to eat another time.

Gorillas get most of the water they need from the leaves they eat.

Gorillas usually sit down to eat. They pick up their food with their fingers and put it into their mouth.

Zoo gorillas enjoy chocolate eggs once in a while.

Zoo gorillas are given plenty of fruit and leaves to eat. In the wild, gorillas feed on as many as 200 different kinds of plants, so they need a lot of variety in the zoo, too. Grapes, oranges, and bananas are favorites of zoo gorillas.

Family life

Gorillas live in family groups. A family usually includes a full-grown male and perhaps a younger male, a few females, and their young of different ages. The oldest male gorilla leads the family. He's called a silverback, because from the age of about 15 he has a patch of silvery-white hair on his back.

A big silverback gorilla watches over and protects his family.

Zoos used to keep gorillas alone or in pairs. Today, zoos prefer to keep gorillas in families as in the wild.

The silverback male decides what the family will do each day—where they will feed and when they will stop to rest. The gorillas usually live very peacefully together. If there are any fights, the silverback settles them with a quick slap or a fierce look.

The other family members respect the silverback and always obey him.

Keeping in touch

Gorillas make many different sounds as they go about their daily lives. As they walk and feed, they make friendly grunts to each other. If they're worried or upset, they may scream, bark, or make roaring noises.

Different groups of gorillas usually stay away from each other. If a strange gorilla comes near a family, the adults will make lots of noise to scare it off, particularly if it's a male. The big silverback may stand up and beat his chest to warn the other gorilla to leave.

Gorillas beat their chests with open hands, not fists.

Gorillas in a family
greet each other
when they meet.

Gorillas also make different faces to
show how they feel. A gorilla opens
its mouth and shows its teeth to
look fierce and scare off a gorilla
from another group.

Although they are usually
gentle, gorillas can look scary
when they bare their teeth.

19

Gorilla babies

A gorilla usually has her first baby when she is about 10 years old. The newborn baby is about half the size of a human baby and very helpless.

For the first few months, the baby stays close to its mother. It clings tightly to her fur or lies cradled in her arms. When it's about four months old, the baby starts to walk on all fours.

A baby gorilla feeds on its mother's milk for at least two years. It starts to eat some

A baby gorilla has a strong grip and holds on tight to its mother as she moves around and feeds.

If a mother gorilla in the zoo can't or won't feed her baby, keepers give the little gorilla a bottle of formula milk—just like human babies drink. Otherwise, the keepers let the mother care for her baby just as she would in the wild.

plants, too, when it is a few months old.

At night, a baby gorilla cuddles up to its mother. It continues to share its mother's bed until her next baby comes along.

A gorilla cradles her baby in her arms while it is feeding on her milk.

21

Growing up

When a young gorilla is about a year old,
it starts to ride on its mother's back as
she travels around. It can find some food
for itself but hasn't yet figured out how to
handle difficult foods such as prickly plants.

Young gorillas like to explore and find out about their surroundings.

A young gorilla soon discovers which plants are good to eat.

During the second year of its life, the young gorilla learns much more about finding the right plants to eat. Gorillas learn by copying their mother and the other gorillas in the family.

It's important for a young gorilla to stay close to its mother. Many youngsters are killed by animals such as leopards.

Playtime

Young gorillas love to play. They wrestle and chase other youngsters in the family. The grunting noises they make as they fight may sound fierce, but it's all in fun. They like to climb and jump in the trees, too.

Even a big male gorilla is surprisingly patient when the young climb over him while he's resting.

Some zoos give gorillas toys to play with. They may give them balls, ropes, barrels, and climbing frames.

Wrestling is a fun game for young gorillas.

Playing is important for young gorillas. It helps make their muscles strong. Young males will also practice beating their chests—just like they've seen their fathers do. One day they'll have to defend their own families.

Leaving home

When a female gorilla is about eight years old, it's time for her to leave her mother and family. She'll soon be ready to have her own baby.

She might find another group to join right away, or she may team up with a male to start a new family group.

Many zoo gorillas have given birth to babies. When the young gorillas are old enough, they are usually taken to another zoo to join a different group and have young of their own.

A young male gorilla usually stays with his family until he is about 12 years old. He may wander by himself for a year or two until he finds a female or a family to join.

It can be hard for a young male to find a family to join, and he may have to fight other males to win a place.

Gorilla fact file

Here is some more information about gorillas. Your mom and dad might like to read this so you can talk about gorillas some more when you see them at the zoo, or perhaps you can read these pages together.

Gorilla

A gorilla is a mammal. It belongs to a group of animals called primates. This group also includes monkeys, baboons, chimpanzees, and orangutans. There are two main kinds of gorillas—western gorillas and eastern gorillas. All gorillas eat plants.

Where gorillas live

The western gorilla lives in western Africa. The eastern gorilla lives in central Africa. Some eastern gorillas live in the mountains in this area. These gorillas are called mountain gorillas.

Gorilla numbers

There are far fewer gorillas in the wild now than there were 10 years ago. Experts think that there are only about 5,000 eastern gorillas and 350 mountain gorillas left. Some people think that there may be as many as 90,000 western gorillas, but there are probably far fewer. Many have been killed by poachers, and in some places, gorillas' homes have been destroyed or disturbed by war.

Size

Gorillas are big, heavy animals. Male gorillas weigh 300 to 600 pounds (135–275 kg), and females weigh about 150 to 310 pounds (70–140 kg). When standing upright, a gorilla is about 3 to 5.7 feet (1–1.75 m) tall.

Find out more

If you want to learn more about gorillas, check out these Web sites:

Dian Fossey Gorilla Fund
http://www.dianfossey.org/home.html

National Geographic.com Kids: Mountain Gorillas
http://www.nationalgeographic.com/kids/creature_feature/0007/gorillas.html

World Wildlife Fund: Gorillas
http://www.worldwildlife.org/gorillas

ARKive Images of Life on Earth
http://www.arkive.org/species/GES/mammals/Gorilla_beringei/more_moving_images.html

Glossary

Ape
A large, tailless animal in the primate group of mammals. Chimpanzees, orangutans, and gorillas are all apes.

Enclosure
The area where an animal lives in the zoo.

Groom
Comb and clean the fur.

Hammock

A length of material that hangs from supports at both ends and can be used as a bed.

Mammal

A warm-blooded animal, usually with four legs and at least some hair on its body. Female mammals feed their babies with milk from their own body.

Poacher

Someone who hunts an animal illegally.

Primate

A group of mammals that includes monkeys and apes.

Index

Africa 6, 28
apes 4, 30
baby gorillas 20–21, 26, 27
chest beating 18, 25
families 8, 16, 17, 18, 23, 24, 25, 26, 27
food 4, 5, 6, 10, 11, 14, 15, 20–21, 22, 23, 28
kinds of gorillas 6, 28
life span 9
moving 10, 11, 12, 14, 22
nests 9, 13
playing 8, 13, 24, 25
population 28
silverback 16–17, 18
size 4, 5, 20, 29
sleeping 9, 13, 21
sounds 18, 24